W9-ASE-802

BUFFALO BILL CODY

FAMOUS FIGURES OF
THE AMERICAN FRONTIER

BILLY THE KID

BUFFALO BILL CODY

CRAZY HORSE

DAVY CROCKETT

GEORGE CUSTER

WYATT EARP

GERONIMO

JESSE JAMES

ANNIE OAKLEY

SITTING BULL

BUFFALO BILL CODY

CHARLES J. SHIELDS

CHELSEA HOUSE PUBLISHERS
PHILADELPHIA

Produced for Chelsea House by
OTTN Publishing, Stockton, NJ

CHELSEA HOUSE PUBLISHERS
Editor in Chief: Sally Cheney
Associate Editor in Chief: Kim Shinners
Production Manager: Pamela Loos
Art Director: Sara Davis
Series Designer: Keith Trego

First Printing

1 3 5 7 9 8 6 4 2

The Chelsea House World Wide Web address is
http://www.chelseahouse.com

Library of Congress Cataloging-in-Publication Data

Shields, Charles J., 1951-
Buffalo Bill Cody / Charles J. Shields.
    p.   cm. – (Famous figures of the American frontier)
Includes bibliographical references and index.
Summary: Examines the life and times of the frontiersman
whose many careers included Pony Express rider, Indian
fighter, scout, and star of his own Wild West Show.
    ISBN 0-7910-6497-2 (alk. paper)
    ISBN 0-7910-6498-0 (pbk.: alk. paper)
1. Buffalo Bill, 1846-1917–Juvenile literature. 2. Pioneers–
West (U.S.)–BiographyJuvenile literature. 3. Frontier and pio-
neer life–West (U.S.)–Juvenile literature. 4.
Entertainers–United States–Biography–Juvenile literature. 5.
Buffalo Bill's Wild West Show–History–Juvenile literature. 6.
West (U.S.)–Biography–Juvenile literature. [1. Buffalo Bill,
1846-1917. 2. West (U.S.)–Biography.] I. Title. II. Series.

F594.B94 S55 2001
978.02'092–dc21
[B]   2001028845

CONTENTS

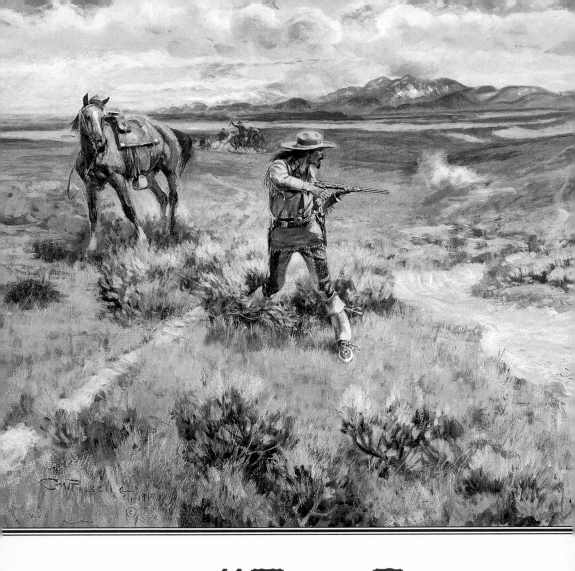

"THE FIRST SCALP FOR CUSTER!"

Buffalo Bill's Duel with Yellowhand is the title of this 1917 painting by well-known Western artist Charles M. Russell. Buffalo Bill Cody later said he shot the Cheyenne Indian in revenge for the deaths of George Custer and his Seventh Cavalry a few weeks earlier.

Lieutenant Colonel George Armstrong Custer of the Seventh *Cavalry* regiment was dead. Custer had been a West Point graduate, a dashing brigadier general at the age of 23 during the Civil War, and, some even said, a first-rate candidate for president—but all that was over now.

On June 25, 1876, at a practically unheard-of spot in

the Montana territory called the valley of the Little Bighorn River, 2,000 Sioux and Cheyenne warriors slaughtered Custer and 210 of his men in the Seventh Cavalry. The battle was a ferocious, one-hour fight; afterward, the nation seethed with hatred for Indians and called for revenge.

One man—William Frederick "Buffalo Bill" Cody—was the first to avenge Custer's death.

Legend has it that when news of Custer's death reached New York, Cody was performing in a loosely autobiographical play about his life as a hunter, scout, and Indian fighter. At the conclusion of the last scheduled performance, Buffalo Bill announced to the audience that he was returning to the West to take an Indian scalp in Custer's honor. The audience yelled its approval.

The truth is that Cody had already closed out his performances earlier in the spring. Weeks before Custer's defeat, Cody was back on the job as an army scout, guiding the Fifth Cavalry as it scoured Wyoming and Nebraska for Indians. On July 7, Cody himself announced the news about the fight at Little Bighorn River to the astonished officers of the Fifth. Cody told them bluntly, "Custer and five companies of the Seventh [were] wiped out of existence."

This 19th-century lithograph shows the popular view of the Battle of the Little Bighorn—Custer standing, firing pistols futilely as the soldiers of the U.S. Seventh Cavalry are overwhelmed by a horde of Sioux warriors. Custer's defeat in the 1876 battle came as a great shock to many Americans.

Rumors spread fast among the soldiers. Word had it that thousands of Indians were planning to bolt from the Red Cloud *reservation* and join Chief Sitting Bull, one of the leaders of the Little Bighorn fight. If that were true, the annihilation of Custer's Seventh Cavalry might be just the beginning.

For the next 10 days, the wary Fifth Cavalry rode hard and kept a sharp lookout. They were guided by 30-year-old Cody.

Around dawn on July 17, as the regiment camped near War Bonnet Creek in Nebraska, a corporal interrupted everyone's drowsy breakfast of coffee and biscuits by shouting, "Look, Lieutenant— there's your Indians!"

Miles away, barely visible across the sandy plains, dozens of mounted Cheyenne warriors were threading down a ravine. Separately, a band of seven Indians appeared unaware of the soldiers observing them; instead, they were watching like

William Cody, pointing out the location of a Sioux camp, is on the left in this photo taken in South Dakota. Next to him is General Nelson A. Miles, who led the American cavalry against the Sioux after the Battle of the Little Bighorn.

fascinated cats a military supply **wagon train** farther west. Ahead of the wagons, two soldiers rode by themselves. As the regiment looked on, the band of seven began urging their horses forward to pick off the soldiers in the lead.

> The admiring wife of one Fifth Cavalry soldier described Buffalo Bill Cody as the troops left their fort. Cody was "straight and slender, with his scarlet shirt belted in and his long hair distinguishing him," she wrote.

Only Cody kept a cool head. He suggested to the regimental commander that rather than chase the Indians away, why not let half a dozen men–himself included–intercept the smaller group before they reached the wagon train? Meanwhile, the Fifth could mount up and prepare a full-scale charge against the rest. The commander agreed with the plan.

Cody and his fellow riders circled around a hill, planning to surprise the Indians descending on the wagon train. But Cody, mounted on a powerful horse, outran his companions and came around the hill alone. As he did, he came face to face with a young Cheyenne warrior wearing a feather **headdress** that nearly touched the ground. Instantly, the two fired at each other. The Indian's pony was hit and fell, while Cody's horse stumbled in a prairie dog hole, pitching its rider forward onto the ground. Another bullet nearly grazed Cody's ear as he knelt, fired, and shot the young Cheyenne in the face. Drawing out his *bowie knife*—or so he later told awestruck audiences of his Wild West Show—he went over to his dead enemy and scalped him "in about five seconds."

When the Fifth Cavalry rode up in force, Cody raised the grisly scalp high and exulted, "The first scalp for Custer!"

Back east, newspapers trumpeted the news of Cody's showdown with a "savage redskin." Another scout, Baptise "Little Bat" Garnier, happily filled reporters' notebooks with details. According to Garnier, the dead warrior was the notorious Yellow Hair. (Actually, the warrior was someone else—Yellow Hand.) Cody's victory would make all the Indians turn tail and run, Garnier assured the press.

Meanwhile, Cody wrote his wife, Louisa, the next day: "We have had a fight. I killed Yellow Hand, a Cheyenne chief, in a single-handed fight. [I am going to] send the war bonnet, shield, bride [bridle], whip, arms and his scalp. . . . I have only one scalp I can call my own: that fellow I fought single-handed in sight of our command, and the cheers that went up when he fell was deafening."

Unfortunately, the gift box arrived before the letter. When Mrs. Cody opened it and found someone's bloody scalp inside, she fainted.

The story of Buffalo Bill Cody versus Yellow Hand mushroomed into a tall tale of American folklore, like how Paul Bunyan scooped out the Great Lakes, or Pecos Bill rode an Oklahoma cyclone. Newspapers referred to the bloody deed, hundreds of novels about Buffalo Bill added to it, and scenes in Cody's own Wild West Show reenacted it. From a brutal shoot-out, it ballooned gloriously into an hours-long, hand-to-hand struggle between the champions of two races, while thousands of Cheyenne watched.

On the other hand, maybe Cody's "first scalp for Custer" was just a hoax in the first place. In 1961, in an article for *Frontier Times*, E. S. Sutton, who as a young man met Cody, recalled Buffalo Bill confiding, "I did not fire a shot in the Yellow Hand affair. I never scalped an Indian . . . those were all tall tales. . . . We never believed them and never expected anyone else to. Then along came Buntline [the promoter behind over 500 Buffalo Bill novels]; the public clamored for such tales; . . . and now they are embalmed in history. . . . Anyway, they were good advertising for the show!"

But if that's true, why in 1930 did Congress invite one of the soldiers who had witnessed the fight—by then a retired but well-known lawman—to point out the spot where it had happened? He did so with no trouble, and the government placed two monuments there—one for the Fifth Cavalry and one to memorialize where Buffalo Bill fought and killed Yellow Hand.

What's the real truth?

When it comes to Buffalo Bill Cody, fact is sometimes hard to separate from fiction. Cody became famous because of his exploits in the West. But then with the help of some professionals in show business, he turned events into drama in his Wild West Show, which toured the United States and Europe for years. Audiences thrilled to scenes of war-whooping Sioux Indians, flaming stagecoaches, sharpshooter contests, and even buffalo hunts staged right before their eyes.

Was Cody wrong to bring American history alive, even if he did make up some of it? All of his shows stressed courage, honor, duty, patriotism, and something that was unusual for the times—fair treatment of Native Americans. Was that wrong? Even now, his defenders argue that America's national character would be different if Buffalo Bill had not put the values of the Old West on display.

In addition, he personally spoke out in favor of women's rights, conservation, planned development of the West, and respect for wildlife. In some ways, he was a 19th-century pioneer looking far into the centuries ahead.

And yet, at the end of his life, when he had no money, some said Buffalo Bill was just a *huckster* and a fake who finally ran out of stories to tell.

What's the real truth about Buffalo Bill Cody?

A portrait of Bill Cody as a young man, wearing his uniform as a scout with the U.S. Army. Cody worked as a Pony Express rider and as a wagon driver for the army before becoming a scout on the frontier.

Young Bill and the Pony Express

William Frederick Cody was born in a log cabin on February 26, 1846, near LeClaire, Iowa, on the border of the American *frontier*. Not until later that year did Iowa become a state.

In 1854, when Bill was eight, the family moved to the Kansas territory, which was then becoming a bloody battlefield. The issue creating such tension was whether

Kansas should come into the Union as a "slave" or a "free" state. According to Cody, his father became one of the early fatalities of the conflict.

In his autobiography, Cody said some Kansas men angrily accused his father of being an *abolitionist* who favored freeing the slaves. They pushed him up on top of a box and told him to explain himself. Cody's father said he was not an abolitionist, but he was against extending slavery into Kansas. That wasn't good enough for the crowd. Cody remembered:

> His speech was followed by a wild yell of derision. Men began crowding around him, cursing and shaking their fists. One of them, whom I recognized as Charlie Dunn, an employee of my Uncle Elijah, worked his way through the crowd, and jumped up on the box directly behind father. I saw the gleam of a knife. The next instant, without a groan, father fell forward stabbed in the back. Somehow I got off my pony and ran to his assistance, catching him as he fell. His weight overbore me but I eased him as he came to the ground.

Afterward, men came again and again to the Cody household, threatening to finish off the wounded man. One night Bill sat on the stairs with a gun, expecting to be the only person between his father and those who wanted to murder him.

Not long afterward, Cody's father died, and young Bill started looking for work. He was only 11, but he needed to help out his mother and his handful of brothers and sisters. He took a job as a mounted messenger for a wagon-freight firm in Leavenworth, Kansas. He went to school for a year, then started making trips west with wagon trains as a *wrangler*–an all-purpose animal-handler.

During the next two years Bill prospected for gold during the Pikes Peak gold rush and trapped game in the Rocky Mountains. But neither of these adventures turned out well, so he returned to Leavenworth in 1860.

By that time, the wagon-freight company had become the firm of Russell, Majors, and Waddell. The company's owners had a bold plan. With a railroad not yet stretching from coast to coast, there was a demand for speedy mail delivery across the plains. They called their idea the Pony Express. The route would run from St. Joseph, Missouri, to Sacramento, California, a distance of about 1,800 miles. It would take about 10 days for the mail to travel the distance. Riders changed horses every 10 to 15 miles, and rode about 75 miles before handing off the mail to the next rider. To attract messengers, the firm put an advertisement in newspapers for "skinny, expert riders willing to risk death daily."

Bill, who had just turned 15, put in for the job and was hired.

The Pony Express captured the popular imagination as romantic and typically "American." Riders encountered hostile Indians, rest stations that had been burned, and relief riders who had been killed or wounded. But still they rode on. Cody later wrote

A Pony Express rider is waved on his way. The fastest trip came in March 1861, when riders carried copies of President Abraham Lincoln's inaugural address to California in 7 days and 17 hours.

about his adventures with pride.

One day he galloped into the station at Three Crossings to find that his relief had been killed in a drunken fight the night before. There was no one to take his place, and his route was 85 miles across the country to the west. Bill had no time to think it over. Selecting a good pony out of the stables, he was soon on his way.

> The Pony Express carried 34,753 pieces of mail during its 18 months of operation. Letters were written on thin paper and cost $5 per half-ounce (reduced to $1 in July 1861). Unfortunately, the Pony Express was a financial failure, losing more than $200,000.

He arrived at Rocky Ridge, the end of the route, on schedule, then turned back to his starting place. The round trip was 322 miles; Bill had made it in 21 hours and 40 minutes.

The Pony Express lasted only 18 months–from April 3, 1860, to November 18, 1861. The entire time it was plagued by bandits on the road, Indian attacks, and shoot-outs involving riders. The business never made a dime, and the firm of Russell, Majors, and Waddell ended in bankruptcy.

During the early part of the Civil War (1861-1865) Cody rode with pro-Union Kansas *guerrilla* outfits. Then, in February 1864, he enlisted with the Seventh Kansas Cavalry in the regular army. He served 19 months as a *teamster*—a driver of horses—and saw action in Tennessee, Mississippi, and Missouri.

Near the end of the war, a friend introduced him to a cousin, Louisa Frederici. As she recalled their meeting, 22-year-old Louisa was completely unnerved when she met 19-year-old Private Cody. He was, she said:

> about the handsomest man I had ever seen! I never knew until that evening how wonderful the blue uniform of the common soldier could be. Clean-shaven, the ruddiness of health glowing in his cheeks; graceful, lithe, smooth in his movements and in the modulations of his speech, he was quite the most wonderful man I had ever known and almost bit my tongue to keep from telling him so.

Bill and Louisa were married on March 6, 1866. Unfortunately, they did not realize until too late that their personalities and temperaments were direct opposites. Louisa wanted a pleasant, orderly, and traditional home; Bill had other plans.

For a short time after they were married, Cody worked as a scout and dispatch carrier out of Fort

Union and Confederate forces clash at the Battle of Franklin, Tennessee—one of many skirmishes in which Bill Cody participated during the Civil War.

Ellsworth, Kansas, where he met up with an old friend from Pony Express days, James "Wild Bill" Hickok. Next, Bill tried his hand at running a hotel, but it failed. He went into the wagon-freight business, but Indians stole his equipment.

Finally, he signed on with Kansas Pacific Railroad as a hunter of buffalo to feed track layers as they made their way across the plains.

The legend of Buffalo Bill was about to begin.

It was not uncommon for trains on the Kansas Pacific Railroad to stop so that passengers could get out and shoot herds of buffalo for sport, as this 1871 lithograph shows. As a hunter for the Kansas Pacific, Cody killed more than 4,000 of the animals in less than a year and a half, acquiring the nickname "Buffalo Bill."

AMERICA MEETS "BUFFALO BILL"

In 1867, the construction crews of the Kansas Pacific Railroad were laying down track over the plains, day after day. The railroad company probably could have shipped food to the workers using the very rails at their feet, but with wild game available everywhere, hiring hunters to supply food was cheaper. Chief on the menu in the railroad camps was buffalo meat.

The animal the Americans called a buffalo is actually a bison. A bison has 14 pairs of ribs—one more than a true buffalo, such as the black buffalo of India. When Europeans arrived in North America, bison were thundering over the land between the Appalachian Mountains and the Rocky Mountains in herds numbering thousands, even millions. Native Americans depended on bison meat for food and bison skins for clothing.

In 1850, an estimated 20 million bison still lived on the western plains. Because of their enormous size but docile behavior, the herds of bison became "easy pickings" for hunters equipped with firearms. By 1889, only 541 of the animals could be found alive in the United States.

By his own count, Cody killed 4,280 head of buffalo in 17 months. He may have won the name "Buffalo Bill" in an eight-hour shooting match with a hunter named William Comstock; they were determining which one deserved the nickname.

Cody's job as a buffalo hunter lasted only a year and a half. By 1868, he returned to work again as a scout for the army, a job he kept until 1872.

Scouts were usually employed only when they were needed, but General Phil Sheridan was so

W. B. "Bat" Masterson, a frontier lawman and buffalo hunter himself, described Bill Cody's stylish way of hunting for the railroad:

> Pistol in both hands, reins in teeth Cody, in those days, used pistols altogether in killing buffalo. He would ride his horse full tilt into a herd of buffalo and, with a pistol in either hand and the bridle reins between his teeth, was almost sure to bring down the day's supply of meat at the first run. With six shots in each pistol, he had often killed as many as eight buffalo on a run. This feat was never equaled, although many times attempted by men who fancied they could ride and shoot as well as Cody.

impressed with Cody that he tried to keep him on the payroll as a regular member of the military. Cody acquired a reputation for his total recall of the vast terrain he traveled, his understanding of Indian culture, and his personal courage and endurance. As chief of scouts for the Fifth Cavalry, Cody took part in 16 battles. For his service, he was awarded the Congressional Medal of Honor in 1872.

Cody first began to receive national attention in 1869, when a newspaper ad announced that the first installation of a new *dime novel*, *Buffalo Bill, The King of Border Men,* would appear in the December 23 issue of the magazine *New York Weekly.*

Dime novels literally cost 10 cents. Printed on cheap paper with a binding made of glue, no one treated them as great literature. But a writer and publisher named Ned Buntline recognized them as the perfect way to satisfy the public's appetite for action-filled stories.

Ned Buntline was the pen name of E. Z. C. Judson, portions of whose own life would have made a good adventure novel. Born in Stamford,

Bill Cody's fame spread thanks to dime novels and magazines such as *Buffalo Bill Stories*. Ned Buntline (above) penned some 200 stories about Buffalo Bill's frontier adventures.

New York, in 1823, Judson served as a cabin boy in the U.S. Navy and rose to the rank of midshipman. (A buntline is a rope fastened to the bottom of a sail.) After he left the navy in 1844, Judson struggled as a writer until he established a sensational newspaper called *Ned Buntline's Own.* In 1849, he caused a riot in New York City, which landed him in prison for a year. When the Civil War broke out, he enlisted in the Union Army, but was dishonorably discharged in 1864 for drunkenness.

Things began looking up for Ned Buntline, however, when he met Buffalo Bill in the fall of 1869. The two men met while Cody was scouting for the army; Buntline was passing through the territory, giving a series of lectures on the dangers of alcohol abuse. In Cody, Buntline recognized a folk hero in the making, someone like Daniel Boone or Kit Carson. In short order, he cranked out a dime novel that made Cody look like a knight in buckskins— *Buffalo Bill, The King of Border Men.*

The Buffalo Bill who appeared in dime novels was always on the side of right, strictly honest, loyal, considerate to others, but quick with a gun if necessary. Although Buntline played with the facts, those who knew Cody said the real man was similar to the fictional hero. Bat Masterson wrote that Cody "had been known on more than one occasion to take a swaggering bully by the neck and, after relieving him of his lethal decorations [weapons], soundly shake him until he promised to behave himself."

The reading public loved the character. Buntline wrote a few other Western novels, not all of them about Cody. But then in 1872 he wrote and produced a play based on Cody's life called *The Scouts of the Plains*, co-starring Buntline and another well-known scout, John B. "Texas Jack" Omohundro.

The play opened in Chicago in December 1872 and was a hit. Buntline convinced Cody to star as himself. The play grew into a full-fledged traveling theater company that toured for 10 years. Cody continued to star in spin-offs such as *Buffalo Bill at Bay, or The Pearl of the Prairie* and *Twenty Days, or Buffalo Bill's Pledge*, featuring Sioux Indians in the cast. Meanwhile, another writer, Prentiss Ingraham, took over the job of writing Buffalo Bill dime novels, eventually producing hundreds of titles.

For the first few years, Cody acted in the winter and scouted in the summer. But how good an actor was he? One critic described him as "a good-looking fellow, tall and straight as an arrow, but

2d SILVER BENEFIT.

McClellan Opera House,
One Night Only.

Saturday Evening, April 3d.

THE ONLY AND ORIGINAL

BUFFALO BILL

HON. W. F. CODY,

Late Chief of the Scouts of the U. S. Army,
and his MAMMOTH COMBINATION
in his great Sensational Drama, entitled,

"The Prairie Waif,"

Introducing the Western Scout and Daring Rider,
Buck Taylor, King of the Cowboys.
A Genuine Band of Pawnee Indians,
Under Pawnee Billy, Boy Chief and Interpreter.
24 First Class Artists.   New and Beautiful Scenery

Mr. Cody, "Buffalo Bill," will give an exhibition of fancy Rifle Shooting,
holding his rifle in twenty different positions, in which he is acknowledged preeminent.
Prices of admission as usual.   Reserved seats, one dollar,
to be had at Forbes & Stromberg's.

Buffalo Bill quickly became a popular stage performer. This poster is from a play he acted in titled *The Prairie Waif.* According to the poster, Cody also gave a shooting exhibition at the performance in Georgetown.

ridiculous as an actor." Nevertheless, his sincerity and good humor shone through. He charmed audiences. As he became a celebrity, the press began taking note of his comings and goings. Foreign ***dignitaries*** such as Grand Duke Alexis, as well as wealthy Easterners, engaged Cody as their personal guide on hunting trips out west.

Gradually, William F. Cody was becoming a living legend as Buffalo Bill. He may not have been a professional actor, but he was learning how to put on a show.

BUFFALO BILL'S WILD WEST
AND CONGRESS OF ROUGH RIDERS OF...

THE WILD WEST
SHOW

A colorful poster from 1899 advertises the Wild West Show, featuring Buffalo Bill on horseback at the right.

Buntline and Cody's partnership in the production of *The Scouts of the Plains* didn't last long. The breakup was the first of several between Cody and business partners. Soon after Cody joined the cast, Buntline retired to Stamford, New York, where he continued to write adventure fiction, compose hymns, and deliver lectures on alcohol abuse.

Meanwhile, Cody managed the theater troupe alone. Another well-known army scout joined the cast–Cody's old friend Wild Bill Hickok. Hickok had been drifting through the West as a gambler after getting a reputation as a trigger-happy sheriff. He performed in the play as himself until 1876.

> After leaving *Scouts of the Plains*, Wild Bill Hickok decided to look for gold. He went to the town of Deadwood in the Montana Territory, hoping to strike it rich. He was shot and killed in a saloon in August 1876 while playing poker. His cards—a pair of eights and aces—still go by the nickname the "dead man's hand."

The continued success of the theater troupe, and the popularity of dime novels featuring Buffalo Bill, proved to Cody that Americans were hungry for drama about the West. The truth was that the fabulous Old West of shoot-outs, Indian raids, buffalo hunts, and the Pony Express was rapidly fading. There was no frontier left; a railroad that linked the East and West coasts had been finished in 1869. Native Americans had been forced onto reservation lands, and buffalo were almost extinct. But most Americans clung to romantic ideas about the lands and people beyond the Mississippi River.

The enormous appeal of the glamorous Old West revealed itself unexpectedly to Cody in the summer of 1882. On a visit to North Platte, Nebraska, Cody learned that the town had no plans for the Fourth of July. He volunteered to serve as chairman of a last-minute festival. Someone suggested calling the event the "Old Glory Blowout." Rather than put on the usual outdoor rodeo show, however, Cody rounded up a stagecoach, some cowboys and Indians, and a small buffalo herd. He also arranged for horse races and shooting contests.

Spectators from miles around descended on North Platte to see the show. Even though there were already nearly 50 circuses traveling the United States, the crowds were so large that the town had difficulty coping with the mob of people who wanted to see the "real West."

All that fall and winter–Cody's last season on the stage–he made plans to duplicate the success of the "Old Glory Blowout." The following spring, Cody and a new partner, a sharpshooter named Doc Carver, presented "The Wild West, Rocky Mountain and Prairie Exhibition" outdoors on the Omaha, Nebraska, fairgrounds. It featured all the drama and excitement that audiences wanted–

a bareback pony race between Pawnee Indians, a sharpshooting demonstration, a battle scene, and even a "startling and soul-stirring attack on the Deadwood mail-coach" by war-whooping Indians. Cody and Doc Carver came riding in to the rescue, guns blazing.

The only trouble was the influence of alcohol. Cody and some of the performers celebrated the opening of the show by drinking; they toasted its success with more drinking; and as the show traveled on to other locations, they hurt the quality of the performances by their continued drinking.

Then Cody suffered a personal loss that seemed to make his alcohol abuse worse. His marriage to Louisa, rarely a happy one, was in trouble. To make matters worse, in October 1883 one of their three daughters died. Carver found Cody in an Omaha hotel nearly senseless from liquor. He told Cody he couldn't put up with his behavior any longer and wanted out of the show. They flipped a silver dollar to divide up the equipment. Carver stormed out, and the two men became enemies for life.

Cody found a new partner, Nate Salsbury, who had a strong track record as manager of a successful theater troupe. In 1884 "Buffalo Bill's Wild West"

A large arch advertising Buffalo Bill's Wild West Show spans a New York City street in this 1884 photo. Cody is on horseback near the center of the photo; his business partner Nate Salsbury is pictured to the right wearing a top hat.

premiered in St. Louis. It was bigger, better rehearsed, and more exciting to watch than anything of its kind.

For three hours, audiences saw a spectacle that was half circus, half history lesson. The spectacle included live elk, cattle, and bison. Former Pony Express riders leaped from one horse to another. A band of Indians attacked a settler's cabin. Cowboys staged a buffalo hunt. Buffalo Bill drove a Wells Fargo stagecoach at full speed into the arena, firing at pursuers. The climax came with a reenactment of Custer's Last Stand at the Little Bighorn in which some Lakota Sioux who had actually fought in the battle played a part.

The next year, 1885, Cody stunned audiences—and the newspapers—by making his show even more amazing. He asked a famous figure in Western history to join the show—solemn, dignified Chief Sitting Bull, who had ordered the counterattack on

Buffalo Bill and Sitting Bull pose together in this photo taken in Montreal, Canada, in 1885. For several years Sitting Bull was one of the main attractions of the Wild West Show.

Custer. In each show, Cody walked with Sitting Bull into the arena and stood beside him in friendship.

> If you have the opportunity to examine what's called a "buffalo nickel," take a look at the Indian's face on the front. The person who posed for it was Iron Tail, one of Buffalo Bill's performers.

Was he going too far? Most Americans despised Sitting Bull, and if they turned out to see the famous Indian, they did so out of hatred. Was Cody using Indians in a shameful way?

Cody never denied that having Indians in his cast was a major attraction. They helped sell tickets. But meeting Sitting Bull may have influenced Cody. After the chief joined the show, Cody remarked: "The defeat of Custer was not a massacre. The Indians were being pursued by skilled fighters with orders to kill. For centuries they had been hounded from the Atlantic to the Pacific and back again. They had their wives and little ones to protect and they were fighting for their existence." On posters for the Wild West Show, Sitting Bull was headlined "An American." Cody may have influenced public opinion by showing Native Americans more respect than they had ever before publicly received.

Most white Americans in the late 1800s felt only mistrust and hostility toward Indians. Years of ***propaganda*** about "red savages" had convinced practically everyone that Native Americans had no worthwhile culture. So when Cody, with the advice of Native Americans, included scenes in the show such as "Indians and Squaws Set Up Camp," "Buffalo Hunt," and "Scenes from Indian Life," audiences saw Indians cast in a different light. There were even staged episodes showing Indians being driven from their homes. At the conclusion of the Wild West shows, audience members had the

Cody would not hire whites to play Indians. "I can put a pair of boots, a bit hat, and a red shirt on any man, call him a cowboy," Cody once told a reporter, "but I cannot dress anyone up and call him an Indian." Each year he hired between 40 and 120 Native Americans. At first he hired from many tribes, but he eventually found that such mixing caused much intertribal conflict. Therefore, in 1891 Cody began a policy of hiring mostly from a single tribe, the Oglala Sioux. In the opening ceremonies of the show, he insisted that the Sioux be the first group to enter the stadium behind him— a place of honor.

opportunity to meet and talk with the Indian performers in their private tepees. These traveling villages not only satisfied visitors' curiosity, but for most Americans, this was the first time they had ever even met an Indian.

On the other hand, the dramatic roles Indians played in the show were generally ones that supported some prejudices about them, too. Acts like the Indian horseback races portrayed Native Americans as a wild people who rode fiercely across the plains. And what were audiences to make of scenes showing Indians attacking stagecoaches, settlers' cabins, and soldiers?

The treatment of cowboys in the Wild West Show paralleled the show's presentation of Native Americans. It's hard to believe now, but at one time the term "cow-boy" was an insult. Thanks in large part to Cody, however, cowboys became popular. Demonstrations in the Wild West Show of bronco riding, calf roping, and other skills wound up being displayed in rodeos across the country.

A performer in the show who became not just famous, but legendary, was Annie Oakley. Born Phoebe Ann Moses in Darke County, Ohio, in 1860, she was called Annie by her sisters. When she was five, her father died after being caught in a snowstorm. For two years she lived in an orphanage, then with a foster family who mistreated her. She eventually returned to her mother.

Practicing with her father's rifle, she learned to shoot so well that she supported her family by supplying game to a hotel in Cincinnati. In a shooting contest at a club, she met Frank Butler, a champion shot, and beat him. They were married two years later. Butler became her manager, and she changed her professional name to Oakley. At 25, she joined the Wild West Show, and she soon became one of the most popular attractions.

Annie Oakley's trick shots included snuffing out candles, shooting accurately over her shoulder by looking into the shiny blade of a bowie knife, and hitting targets tossed in the air.

In 1887, Oakley traveled to Europe, the first of several tours for the Wild West Show abroad. Each day, 30,000 to 40,000 people came to glimpse the American western frontier. The high-spirited, five-foot-tall Oakley fascinated Queen Victoria, and the London Gun Club welcomed her as its first female guest. In Vienna, she arranged a charity event for orphans. She was so popular everywhere,

Phoebe Ann Moses Butler, better known as Annie Oakley, took her professional name, Oakley, from the name of a Cincinnati suburb. Chief Sitting Bull, whom she taught to write, called her "Mochin Watanya Cicilla," which meant "my daughter, little sure shot." She became known as "Little Sure Shot" ever after.

in fact, that Buffalo Bill became jealous, and soon began giving her a hard time. After that, she and her husband stayed away from the show for two years.

In many ways, however, Cody was an unusually open-minded man for his times. The pay scale in the Wild West Show was not based on gender. "If a woman can do the same work that a man can do and do it just as well," he remarked, "she should have the same pay." When a woman reporter asked him whether he thought the majority of women were qualified to vote, Cody answered, "As well qualified as the majority of men."

Boys and girls peek under a tent to see what's happening at the Wild West Show in a photo taken around the turn of the century.

His strongest opinions focused on the West. Despite his own experiences, he deplored the hide-hunters of the 1870s and 1880s who had slaughtered the buffalo, he said, "cruelly, recklessly." He consistently defended American Indians, cautioning the government to "never make a promise to the Indians that is not fulfilled," and blaming outbreaks of violence on "broken promises and broken treaties by the government." All frontier scouts, he said, knew better than to try to trick Indians. "In nine cases out of ten where there is trouble between white men and Indians, it will be found that the white man is responsible. Indians expect a man to keep his word. They can't understand how a man can lie."

Cody also enjoyed children. In photographs of him in costume, sitting with boys and girls beside him, it's no exaggeration to say he is beaming with happiness. The show distributed thousands of free passes to orphanages in the towns where it played. A nine-year-old orphan, Johnny Baker, attached himself to the show and begged to do anything to help. Cody gave him the job of tossing blue glass balls in the air for sharpshooters. Eventually, Cody adopted Baker and taught him to be a sharpshooter in his own right. Baker remained with Cody as his business adviser until the end of Cody's life.

In 1893, "Colonel" Cody—the honorary rank having been given to him by a Nebraska governor—brought the show to the Columbian Exposition in Chicago. Side by side with mammoth exhibitions of America's advances in science, engineering, and technology, Cody's show provided a background on the kind of values Americans liked to associate with their country—courage, creativity, and patriotism, for instance. It was the intersection of America's past and its future.

By the end of the century, Buffalo Bill Cody was one of the best-known and most beloved men in the United States.

In this 1922 oil painting by Robert Lindneux, Buffalo Bill strikes a relaxed pose in the saddle. He is wearing a buckskin jacket ornamented with fringe and colorful beads; the horse's bridle is decorated with shells placed together to form flowers.

CODY'S FINAL YEARS

"All my interests are still with the west—the modern west," Cody wrote near the end of his life. Beginning in the early 1890s, while the Wild West Show was at its peak of popularity, he turned his attention to developing his own farsighted vision of the modern West.

He first rode into the Big Horn Basin of Wyoming in the 1870s and was entranced by its beauty. At that time, only Indians, hunters, trappers, explorers, and mountain men had ever seen it. Not only was the scenery gorgeous, but Cody, with his hunter's eye, recognized it as excellent fishing and game land. The soil was rich but *arid*, although water for *irrigation* was plentiful. Not far away, the federal government established Yellowstone National Park in 1872.

In 1896, Cody and a group of investors formed the Shoshone Land and Irrigation Company. Irrigation was necessary for developing the desert stretches in that northwest corner of Wyoming. The partners also decided the area needed a town to anchor it. Moreover, with Yellowstone only 50 miles away, tourists and hunters would need the kind of services a town could provide. At the urging of his investors, Buffalo Bill agreed to name the site Cody. Streets were laid out and named for General Phil Sheridan and the originators of the community.

Developing raw wilderness and building a town in a remote area is a costly enterprise. But Cody had been an optimist his entire life. He believed that with enough effort, his dreams of the modern Western community would thrive. Unfortunately, his optimism led him into trouble financially.

At first, all the right things were happening to the

town of Cody. By 1900, farms and ranches began appearing in the newly irrigated areas, and the town grew. The Burlington Railroad completed a spur to Cody by 1901—an excellent sign. The railroad could bring visitors from all directions.

Then Buffalo Bill went full throttle financially. In the space of just a few years, he poured his money into the town, building the Irma Hotel—the "Hotel in the Rockies," named for his youngest daughter—and the Wapiti Inn. He also owned the T-E and Carter Ranches, and he had interests in coal mines and gas and oil claims, as well as the Canal Company, Buffalo Bill Barn, Cody Enterprise, and Cody Trading Company.

The development of the area was outstripping the natural resources—and Buffalo Bill's money. He turned to fund-raising, trying to find the money to keep projects moving. When the $2 million he needed for **hydroelectric power** failed to materialize, Colonel Cody persuaded his friend, President Theodore Roosevelt, to build the Shoshone Dam and Reservoir. With the completion of the dam in 1910, the community received all the water and electric power it required.

Also with the assistance of the president, Cody

President Theodore Roosevelt approved construction of a large dam near Cody, Wyoming. When the Shoshone Dam and Reservoir was completed, it was the highest dam in the world. In 1946, it would be renamed the Buffalo Bill Dam and Reservoir.

helped establish the first great national forest, the Shoshone, and the first forest ranger station, located at Wapiti. In Wyoming and Colorado, he worked to establish game preserves and limit hunting seasons. Gifford Pinchot, noted conservationist and head of the Forest Service for Roosevelt, hailed Cody as "not only a fighter but a seer."

Cody kept up a steady drumbeat of publicity for his vision of an ideal Western community, where Old West values and 20th-century technology and prosperity would merge. The Wild West Show encouraged audiences to come out West and settle in Wyoming before it was too late. When the show closed for the season, Cody led investors and foreign visitors on hunting trips that showcased the region's best features.

All in all, the effort must have been exhausting, and Cody began to show the signs of strain, both physically and financially. On his doctor's orders, he finally quit drinking. But the life of a performer on the road is hard, and Cody was no longer young; he turned 60 in 1906. He was in pain whenever Johnny Baker helped him into the saddle so he could ride into an arena, wave to the crowds, and shoot a few targets.

The year 1907 marked a turning point—the Wild West Show began to falter. One of Cody's key financial backers died, and Cody could barely maintain the show with the money that remained. Already Cody's investments in Wyoming were a constant drain on his fortune. Added to this, in 1905 he and Louisa divorced. A lengthy and expensive lawsuit bled his finances still more.

In 1908 he combined his show with Pawnee Bill's under the title "Buffalo Bill's Wild West and Pawnee Bill's Great Far East." To bolster attendance, Cody began a series of farewell tours in 1910, after which he intended to retire to Wyoming. An ad in the *Stockton Evening Mail* of October 8, 1910, reads "Buffalo Bill Positively Bids You Good-By." The tours took nearly three seasons to complete, and troubles befell the show constantly. Cody had overextended himself financially with bad investments, and keeping the show running and managing

Buffalo Bill (right) stares into the camera with a haunted look as his friend Pawnee Bill (G. W. Lillie) writes at a desk. Buffalo Bill's later years were financially difficult, as the popularity of the Wild West Show waned.

activities in Wyoming proved too much.

In 1912 he traveled to Denver to obtain a $20,000 loan for the show, not realizing his *creditor* planned to trap him. When "Buffalo Bill's Wild West and Pawnee Bill's Great Far East" arrived in Denver the following year, the sheriff seized it, saying the loan was due immediately. Cody didn't have the money. He was forced to watch while the last pieces of the Wild West Show were auctioned off.

His creditor still had one more card to play. He was owner of the Sells-Floto Circus. Using the debt as an excuse, he forced Cody to perform in a traveling circus for two unhappy years.

In 1914, however, still looking to the future, Cody became interested in motion pictures. He supervised production of a silent film about the history of the West, only portions of which still survive. (At one point, his Native American friend Iron Tail informed him of "big trouble." The Indian extras planned to use real bullets against the retired cavalry soldiers in the film to avenge the deaths of their ancestors.) The *Washington Post* reported, "Col. Cody is in fine physical condition . . . full of snap and ginger and straight as an arrow."

But Cody's health was declining. By January

1917, he was clearly dying at his sister's home in Denver, Colorado. He asked the doctor attending him how long he had left to live. The doctor sugar-coated his reply, until Cody insisted impatiently, "How long?" The doctor guessed about 36 hours. Cody suggested they just forget about it and play cards. He died on January 10 and was buried on Lookout Mountain near Denver.

Many tributes followed. The chief of the Oglala Sioux sent a telegram expressing the tribe's regret. The California legislature passed a resolution to "express its appreciation of the courage and fear-

---

This telegram from the chief of the Oglala Sioux in Pine Ridge, South Dakota, was sent on January 12, 1917, after the death of Buffalo Bill:

The Oglala Sioux Indians of Pine Ridge, South Dakota, in council assembled, resolve that expression of deepest sympathy be extended by their committee in behalf of all the Oglalas, to the wife, relatives, and friends of the late William F. Cody for the loss they have suffered; that these people who have endured may know that the Oglalas found in Buffalo Bill a warm and lasting friend; that our hearts are sad from the heavy burden of his passing, lightening only in the belief of our meeting before the presence of our Wakan Tanka in the great hunting ground.

–Chief Jack Red Cloud

lessness of this, our last frontiersman, whose life stands forth in the establishment and foundation of our western country." For years after his death, newspapers carried interviews with plainsmen, scouts, soldiers, Indians, and hunters who had some story about Buffalo Bill to share.

In the mid-1920s came a rash of ideas for memorials and museums to honor Buffalo Bill. But almost at the same time, a competing effort surfaced to ruin his memory. A book in 1928 titled *The Nothing of Buffalo Bill* was reviewed in major newspapers. One such review appeared in the *Kansas City Star* on December 16, 1928, and was titled "Stripping the Heroic Legend From Buffalo Bill." A headline in the *Hardin Tribune* of April 5, 1929, read "The Famous Exploits Attributed To Him Were But Press Agent Imagination," although the actual article roundly defended Cody's reputation.

The 1930s saw the end of the large outdoor arena extravaganzas modeled after Buffalo Bill's Wild West, such as the Miller Brothers 101 Ranch Shows, and the short-lived Col. Tim McCoy's Wild West Show. Perhaps audiences' interest waned. After all, silent movies had become "talkies," and audiences could now see the scenery, hear the war

Citizens of Colorado lay a wreath at Buffalo Bill's grave. The former scout, Pony Express rider, and showman remains a fascinating figure to those interested in the American West.

whoops of Indians, and wince at the sound of gunfire from charging cavalry troops in a theater. Without realizing it, however, they were witnessing versions of the Wild West Show, which continue on until today.

The impression of the Old West that Buffalo Bill Cody stamped on Americans' imagination, and on our national character, may be permanent. Small-town rodeos, reenacted cattle drives, dude ranches, reconstructed ghost towns, expressions such as "riding off into the sunset," "cowboys and Indians," "circling the wagons," and "Custer's Last Stand," all live on mainly because millions of people saw Buffalo Bill's Wild West Show. The Western paperback novel—an extension of Ned Buntline's dime novels—is a form of literature that still attracts many readers. The "pioneer spirit," the pride of independence, and some would say the national fascination with guns, all entered the American character because Buffalo Bill glorified them.

In addition, white Americans' first exposure to Native Americans as a people who have a strong and proud identity—not as "red savages"—occurred in countless towns and cities under Cody's show tents. His Indian performers called him "Pahaska," or "Long Hair," and they considered him a friend. Black Elk, who fought as a teenager at the Little Bighorn, spoke of Cody's "strong heart."

Sitting Bull reportedly once grew quite angry when a relative wore a hat that Buffalo Bill had given to him.

"My friend Long Hair gave me this hat," the great Sioux chief boasted. "I value it highly, for the hand that placed it upon my head had a friendly feeling for me."

CHRONOLOGY

1846 William F. Cody is born on February 26

1849 The Codys move to LeClaire, Iowa

1854 The Cody family moves to Kansas after a short stay in Missouri

1857 Isaac Cody, Bill's father, dies; Bill Cody is hired as a messenger for Majors and Russell Co. in Kansas

1860 At the age of 15, Cody becomes a Pony Express rider; makes the third-longest trip–322 miles

1864 Enlists in the Seventh Kansas Volunteer Cavalry

1866 Cody marries Louisa Frederici on March 6

1867 Earns the nickname "Buffalo Bill" as a buffalo hunter for the Kansas Pacific Railroad

1868 Appointed chief of scouts for the Fifth U.S. Cavalry; on a winter campaign Bill leads the rescue of a troop guided by Wild Bill Hickok

1869 Guides the Fifth Cavalry to victory at Summit Springs, Colorado; *Buffalo Bill, The King of the Border Men*, written by Ned Buntline, is published–the first of more than 550 dime novels about Buffalo Bill

1872 Cody wins Medal of Honor; guides buffalo-hunting party and provides "Indian" entertainment for Grand Duke Alexis of Russia; begins 11-season stage career by playing himself in a melodrama of frontier life, *The Scouts of the Plains*

1876 Famous fight with Yellow Hand; produces and stars in *The Red Right Hand; or, Buffalo Bill's First Scalp for Custer*, a dramatization of the War Bonnet Battle

1879 As a public figure, begins speaking out for Indian rights; his autobiography is published

1883 Buffalo Bill presents first Wild West Show in Omaha, Nebraska; this same year, Sitting Bull participates in the last traditional buffalo hunt of the Sioux, as the northern herd is now almost extinct

1884 Annie Oakley joins the Wild West Show

1885 Sitting Bull joins Buffalo Bill's Wild West Show

1887 Cody introduces Europe to the Wild West at the American Exhibition in London

1889 Cody takes the Wild West to France and tours Europe for four years

1893 Wild West opens at the World's Columbian Exhibition in Chicago

1895 -96 Cody spends large sums of money developing town of Cody, Wyoming

1905 Sues his wife for divorce

1908 Merges Wild West Show with Pawnee Bill's Great Far East

1913 Wild West Show goes bankrupt in Denver, Colorado; the Col. W. F. Cody Historical Pictures Company is formed to produce short films on the Native American wars

1916 Cody joins and makes his final appearance with Miller Brothers and Arlington 101 Ranch Wild West

1917 Dies on January 10 in Denver, Colorado; is buried on Lookout Mountain

GLOSSARY

abolitionist–during the 19th century, a person in favor of ending slavery.

arid–land that is excessively dry and does not receive enough rainfall to support farming.

bowie knife–a single-edged hunting knife with the back edge curved to a sharp point; named after James Bowie, a hero in the Texas revolution.

cavalry–an army troop mounted on horses.

creditor–a person to whom a debt is owed.

dignitaries–people who possess high rank, or hold a position of power or honor.

dime novel–an inexpensive book, usually printed on cheap paper, containing sensational or fantastic stories.

frontier–the land at the edge of territory settled by humans.

guerrilla–a form of fighting that uses sabotage and harassment of the enemy forces.

headdress–an elaborate covering for the head. Native American headdresses were often made with feathers.

huckster–a peddler; someone who sells cheap goods.

hydroelectric power–electric power created by using waterpower.

irrigation–the practice of supplying farmland with water by artificial means.

propaganda–ideas, information, or claims (not necessarily true) spread to further a certain cause.

reservation–a piece of public land set aside where Native Americans were forced live.

teamster–a person who drives a team of horses; a wagon driver.

wagon train–a line of wagons traveling together to the American West, carrying either settlers or supplies.

wrangler–an all-purpose animal handler.

Further Reading

Carter, Robert. *The Man Behind the Legend.* New York: John Wiley and Sons, 2000.

Frederiksson, Kristine. *American Rodeo: From Buffalo Bill to Big Business.* College Station, Tex.: Texas A&M University Press, 1993.

Green, Carl, and William R. Sanford. *Buffalo Bill Cody: Showman of the West.* Berkeley Heights, N.J.: Enslow, 1996.

Kasson, Joy S. *Buffalo Bill's Wild West: Celebrity, Memory, and Popular History.* New York: Hill & Wang, 2000.

Martin, Greg. *Buffalo Bill's Wild West: An American Legend.* New York: Random House, 1998.

Sayes, Isabelle S. *Annie Oakley and Buffalo Bill's Wild West.* Mineola, N.Y.: Dover, 1991.

Stevensen, Augusta. *Buffalo Bill: Frontier Daredevil.* New York: Aladdin, 1991.

Wetmore, Helen Cody. *Last of the Great Scouts.* New York: Tor, 1996.

PICTURE CREDITS

CHARLES J. SHIELDS lives in Homewood, a suburb of Chicago, with his wife Guadalupe, an elementary school principal. He has a degree in history from the University of Illinois in Urbana-Champaign, and was chairman of the English department and the guidance department at Homewood-Flossmoor High School in Flossmoor, Illinois.